THE MAKING OF A BALTIMORE ALBUM QUILT

TIMORE ALBUM QUILT

TEXT BY FRANCES BENTON

INTRODUCTION BY MARGARET RAMSEY

PREFACE BY ELLY SIENKIEWICZ

PHOTOGRAPHY BY BEN THORNAL

A MARY ELIZABETH JOHNSON BOOK

BLACK BELT PRESS
MONTGOMERY

A Mary Elizabeth Johnson Book, published by the Black Belt Press,
Post Office Box 551, Montgomery, Alabama 36101.

Photo of Frances on page 15 by Quintin Ellison; courtesy of The Franklin Press, Franklin,
North Carolina.

Design by Breuna Baine.

*The Black Belt, defined by its dark, rich soil,
stretches across central Alabama. It was the
heart of the cotton belt. It was and is a place of
great beauty, of extreme wealth and grinding
poverty, of pain and joy. Here we take our stand,
listening to the past, looking to the future.*

Manufactured in Hong Kong.
Library of Congress Cataloging-in-Publication Data
Benton, Frances, 1922-
    The making of a Baltimore Album quilt /text by Frances Benton; introduction by
Margaret Ramsey; preface by Ellie Sienkiewicz; photographs by Ben Thornal—1st ed.
        p.   cm.
Includes bibliographical references.
ISBN: 1-881320-45-6
    1. Quilting– United States 2. Album quilts–Maryland–Baltimore–History. 3.
Benton, Frances, 1922- –Correspondence.
4. Quiltmakers–United States–Correspondence.   I. Title.
TT835.B3554 1995
746.46' 092–dc20
[B]   95–10425
                                        CIP

CONTENTS

ON MEETING ALBUM QUILTS AND ALBUM MAKERS

by Elly Sienkiewicz

I do not consider myself a mystical person. But years ago an Album block, pictured in a book, slipped into my soul. The book was Safford and Bishop's *America's Quilts and Coverlets* and the block was an épergne of fruit from an antebellum Baltimore Album Quilt.

Beginning in 1975, that block sang gently to me, its tune a cloud shadow brushing almost unnoticed across my path. Though just in snatches, that other-worldly music persisted through my young mother life—a life burdened by a home business become so successful that outdoing myself was exhausting my spirit. In 1979, my neighbor Sue Hannan paused the car in which we were riding at a stoplight and chided, "You don't take time to smell the flowers," when, lightning-fast, a huge tree crashed in the wind down onto my side of the car, pancaked it, and so doing, stole the better part of three years of my life.

When, in late 1982, after that long recovery, Sue asked me to join her at the Baltimore Museum of Art's Album show, I heard the Album block's song begin again. With the song came questions. What gave that appliqué such dimension? Why was its blue so distinctive? Was paint used so that the color glowed so? Why the tidily stitched circles on the fruit? And why, for Goodness' sake, the acorn amongst the fruit? All such technical, formula questions—quiltmaker questions.

A quiltmaker myself, I would go to Baltimore and find the answers by studying the quilts. There, twenty-four antique "Baltimores" spoke to me in a room-resonating song, but it was a song without words. Ever since, I've sought the words to that chorus, the answers to those questions. Now, years later, I'm humbled and probably wiser, not so rigid, worlds happier. I listen to the quilts better, want more simply to understand, rather than to prove something. I have learned the language of the flowers, learned that the acorn symbolizes longevity.

The song of the Albums is not only in the history books, the archives, and the cloth: women's stilled voices hang in the air when one works on an Album. Lifetimes ago, they stitched the feelings wordlessly into that treasured cloth. We today are less reticent, but even we who speak more directly leave silent messages around and about our quilts. Listen to Frances's words. Listen to Frances's quilt.

LONG-AGO GENESIS

The question burns: "Who made the antebellum Baltimore Album quilts and why?" History's evidence increasingly rewards research and much of it is well-corroborated by the quilts. Nonetheless, at this writing, no named authorship has been sufficiently substantiated. The answer to why Baltimore's albums broke onto quiltmaking history with such a brilliant, far-reaching voice has to be in movements, rather than in the identification of an artist's name.

The quilts themselves teach as much about the method of their making as they do about the lives and times of the women who made them. Learning their techniques, then adapting the process to one's own, comes quite naturally to a quiltmaker. To learn from the albums is to become a live strand in a twist of thread reaching back into time and forward into the future. Though quiltmakers like Frances Benton stitch this journey mostly alone at home, they stitch in the close company of the women of old Baltimore, or of their contemporaries who have passed on the patterns or shared fresh designs in the style. They feel attached to those who journey with them: supportive friends like Margaret Ramsey, family, and all those others who simultaneously are journeying beside them to Baltimore—and beyond.

Frances mentions the 1994 Baltimore Album Revival! contest sponsored by my California publisher. She dreams of the prestige of winning, the challenge of competing with highly skilled quiltmakers, and of testing one's own accomplishment against theirs. Album quiltmakers are a sisterhood: some stitch together, meeting once a week or once a month to share progress. Others know through books, journals, and guilds that they are part of a worldwide community sharing something important. Increasingly, Album makers are forming clubs with names like "Good Ladies West of Baltimore," and "Good Ladies of Baltimore, South Africa."

This deep-rooted connectedness of those stitching the Album path fascinates me.

Increasingly, I'm caught by the passion, the vivacity of the women who, like Frances, are driven to express themselves through an Album Quilt. They are so alive! It is through their monumental quilts that we are allowed a glimpse of the fire within.

For me, making an heirloom quilt ensures an earthly immortality—it will leave the work of my hand among the living. Do all quiltmakers think thus? I don't know for sure, but Frances writes, "I hope someone appreciates my work as much as I appreciate those who came before me."

Stitching Revivalist Albums has made antique Baltimore's aesthetic an integral part of me, so much so that the distiction blurs now between what might be called my original design and what of my design is interpretive. Even the unclear line between quilts made by one individual and those quilts clearly group-made echoes what we sense of old Baltimore. Although we might use another's pictures or patterns for inspiration, we nonetheless put so much of ourselves into an Album as to believe that it expresses our feelings perfectly. One can hear this in Frances Benton's words and see it in her passionately wrought Album.

ALBUMS, BALTIMORE ALBUMS, AND REVIVALIST ALBUMS

At some point you, dear reader, may well have asked why that fair port city's name attaches to a whole quilt genre, even when a modern quilt is made a century and more later, and in a state far beyond Maryland. Frances titled her quilt "Baltimore Album" and thereby bestowed upon it both honor and high esteem. A working definition of a classic Baltimore Album would be "appliquéd album quilts made in Baltimore, Maryland in the middle of the nineteenth century."

An album is a collection on a theme, therefore in an album quilt the blocks generally differ from one another while maintaining a similarity of feeling. The Baltimore albums were so numerous and differed so distinctively from quilts that had come before that I believe they were a highly prized, separate genre of "fancy patchwork" quilts, famous abroad in the land, even in their own time.

Why there were so many of them, why this ornate, symbol-filled, labor-intensive style caught on like wind-driven fire in that place at that time is something I've written on extensively.

Increasingly, I believe the style blossomed in the convergence of three movements: the Institutes for the Promotion of the Mechanic Arts, Methodism, and Odd Fellowdom. With apologies, I must refer you to the Recommended Reading List and to my forthcoming [1997] book, *Stitched in Cloth, Carved in Stone.*

In the art and antiques community, a Baltimore Album Quilt is ideally defined by documentable characteristics: time, geography, and appearance. Nomenclature in the quilt field is difficult, and a pat definition is almost impossible for quilts of this type that have been made since the mid-1850s. "Revivalist Baltimores," "New Baltimores," or "Turn of the Twentieth-Century Baltimores" are, by definition, beyond the classic Baltimore Album Quilt in time and place. I believe their blocks must have a clear and recognizable connection to the block styles of classic Baltimores. If they are simply fancy floral-decked appliqué, they are something else. If the blocks have an instantly recognizable connection, but their set is innovatively "new," I'd still call them Revivalist Baltimores.

Among themselves, contemporary quiltmakers simply call the Baltimore-style Album Quilts they make "Baltimore Albums," just as Frances does. With delightful abandon, one can read of Baltimore Albums taught in Amsterdam, Paris, Tokyo, Toronto, or Santa Fe. When the Albums are displayed publicly, some names become more evocative: Lisa McCulley calls hers "Where You Tend a Rose" and Ruth Meyers named hers "Baltimore Beauties for Bob." (Both quilts took prizes in the 1994 Baltimore Album Revival! Show in Lancaster, Pennsylvania.)

These quilts' current revival owes its thanks to the museums where fine examples are housed and to the auction houses and antique dealers from whom private collectors seek Baltimore Albums as the most highly valued of America's antique quilt heritage. The Revivalist Baltimore Albums, of which Frances's is one, began to be made in earnest in the early 1980s. A handful were made a few decades earlier, from a *Woman's Day* magazine pattern of the Metropolitan Museum of Art's finest Baltimore Album.

Since 1983, literally hundreds of Baltimore block patterns have been published. So wide is the selection that innovative combinations, like Frances's, are beginning to give the new Baltimores a distinctive look all their own. Current enthusiasm for these quilts seems so ardent that it is increasingly reflected in quilt books, the Baltimore Beauties fabric line, notions, and a plethora of gift and museum shop items. A second major Baltimore Album Revival! contest scheduled for 1998 has quiltmakers setting their sights ever higher.

My Album books, begun in 1983 with *Spoken Without a Word*, now number ten. This burgeoning could only have happened because the

Albums themselves call irresistibly to modern quiltmakers: they are a challenge and they tug at a quiltmaker's soul. While I am first a quiltmaker, then a writer, I am foremost an appreciator, an avid admirer of the old quilts. I feel, by now, a dear friend, fascinated by them, by their makers, and by the times in which they lived. Those times seem not so different in essence from our times. In many ways, thinking about those women caught in the Industrial Revolution's swirl helps me adjust as we are swept into the Post-Industrial age. Those quilts and their makers speak to me.

Although I earn my livelihood by this love, it is still something precious and inward-turned. It is not too much to say that Baltimore Albums have changed my life. They have become almost a myth for me, and their song aids my understanding of my place in the world. And if this sounds too far-fetched, I think Frances knows what I mean. I hope so, for I feel I know her through her quilt and through those who have stitched this path before her and with her. As for her lively, plain-spoken letters, they have the happy familiarity of communing with a fellow Album-maker.

The Song of the Baltimore Album Quilt

As I write this, night-fallen snow weighs heavily on the arborvitae outside my window. Sunlight floods the amaryllis inside on the sill, washing them so brightly that five flower heads dance with shimmering shades of red. Stitching Album blocks makes me see the world's wonder anew—today I see wee gold-tipped trumpets thrusting from each flower's throat, one center trumpet longer than those around it. I am pleased with myself for having fed my plants recently;

me for pausing from my sewing and writing to tend them. I love my amaryllis, quiet friends whose ability to lift my spirits I cherish.

In 1989, when I was writing *Baltimore Beauties and Beyond, Volume I,* I bought my first three bulbs from the grocery store. Like the books, the bulbs have multiplied, making the string of Februaries since into a stage where nature's beauty wrestles with my drive to stitch and write. What do I love to write about? How the Album Quilts have led me back to smell the flowers, for example.

I know my amaryllis well, know that while the leaves shrivel, yellowed, in the fall, they are nourishing a rich bulb only disguised by drab exfoliation. Both faith and knowledge teach this promise of life renewed. These plants are magical, pot-bound miracles turning brown earth to Victoria green and Turkey red, pink and white in painterly mixtures.

Making a Baltimore Album also takes faith and knowledge. But making an Album involves more work than growing my few house flowers. It is a bigger undertaking and occupies more of the spirit. There's joy to the work—you can read that in Frances's letters. But the joy is also in the challenge, in the reach, in the testing of one's talents. To love the fineness of the famous antique Baltimores is to recognize excellence. There is a song in being able to stitch excellence. It is a song passed along from mother to daughter, teacher to pupil, friend to friend, over the centuries.

The thought comes sometimes that I could die today a happy woman: I've done nothing I regret, and I have lived life to the fullest. I wonder though, could I have said this before that song, sung by an Album block, slipped softly off the page of a book and into my waiting soul?

I'D LIKE YOU TO MEET FRANCES BENTON

by Margaret Ramsey

Editor's note: Mrs. Ramsey was manager from 1979 to 1993 of the Franklin, North Carolina, crafts cooperative known nationwide as MACO Crafts. She and the cooperative acted as Frances Benton's agent, marketing her quilts and, later, her quilt tops. As in any cooperative, a percentage of the proceeds from each sale stayed with the organization to help keep it running. Although Mrs. Ramsey has now turned the job of managing MACO over to someone else, she maintains close ties with the cooperative and maintains her correspondence with Mrs. Benton. MACO and the new manager, Ann Warren, continue to represent Mrs. Benton.

Almost everyone has a picture in their mind of a typical mountain quilter. She is a modest little old lady who quickly and practically twists her grey hair into a bun; she wears a gingham housedress covered by an apron; she certainly never wears any make-up or jewelry that would call attention to herself; she does, however, consistently surprise one and all with the beauty she produces at her quilting frame. As manager of one of the nation's largest craft co-operatives and one of the few specializing in quilts, I have known many quilters who more or less fit that mold, and I have been thrilled by the quilts these "typical mountain quilters" have produced.

However, about fifteen years ago a woman appeared in my office, introduced herself as a quilter, and totally destroyed that stereotype. Yes, she was little, and she was— well, at least, "older," but there any similarity to a typical mountain quilter ended. Her blonde hair was piled high on her head in curls, she was dressed in a pants suit straight off the pages of *Vogue*, and she was wearing rings on about eight fingers. The only thing she had in common with other quilters I had known was the sack full of awe-inspiring quilts she carried. That day—when MACO Crafts discovered Frances Benton, and Frances discovered MACO—was the beginning of a beautiful relationship!

Of the thousands of quilts that pass through MACO, the vast majority are pieced, rather than appliquéd. This is true of most shops, and for a very good reason: piecing is easier to do. Hand appliqué is an art in itself, it is done by very few people, and very rarely done well. When Frances started emptying her "sack" that day, we all realized that we were meeting a master of the art. A customer walked up as we were examining them and said, "Are those pieces glued on there?" That pretty well describes them. Her stitches were, to all appearances, non-existent; every piece lay perfectly flat; there was not a pucker or a thread pulled too tight in any of the quilts. That first encounter assured me of Frances's technical abilities, but, as our friendship grew, I came to know and admire the many facets of this "jewel" of a woman: her originality, her determination, her tremendous courage in facing constant pain, and, most of all, her unfailing and contagious sense of humor. Although she did not start making quilts until later in her life, Frances had learned very early the discipline required for perfection. She describes her first experiences as a quilter:

"My mother was a tyrant and I was very impressionable; therefore, when she yelled, I jumped. To her, you were to be as perfect as you could be, but even that was never enough for her. Of her three girls, I was the only one she trusted to sew anything for her, so I suppose I measured up somewhat. Not everyone did, though . . . my future mother-in-law was in a church group that met at my mother's to quilt for the church fund. (I was about seventeen.) After the group left, mama would take out all my future in-law's stitches and quilt her part over . . . ."

In a few words, Frances summarizes her life "BQ," that is, Before Quilts: "I retired as an assistant treasurer of a thirty-million-dollar mortgage firm at age forty-five, bought a farm and tried to do all the things I felt I had missed out on. Until then, I had done as others wanted, but after age forty-five, I did strictly what I wanted. For a while, I did quite a bit of needlepoint, then discovered quilts and found the calling of my old age."

As Frances's talents developed and expanded, a darker side of her life was, unfortunately, taking shape. For years she suffered with osteoarthritis, which finally disabled her to the point that she could no longer maintain her own home; now she happily shares her daughter's. She is also a "brittle diabetic," which means she has to always carry her little medical kit and constantly monitor her blood sugar. Although this would be enough to stop most of us, it was only the beginning of problems for her. Several years ago she developed a condition which keeps her in constant pain—not a dull ache, but sharp, excruciating pain. (This is in addition to the constant arthritic pain.) Repeated visits to leading specialists and university hospitals have failed to give her a diagnosis—or any relief.

Most people would be completely immobilized by this combination, but, fortunately for all of us, Frances copes with the pain by making quilts! As with all true artists, she completely immerses herself in her project, and this gives her an escape from pain for a little while. She told me once that she loves every part of quiltmaking: pattern drafting, color selection, and assembly. Since she can't sit, or stand, for very long, she keeps several projects in various stages so she can change positions. Incredible as it sounds, she has done many of her appliqué projects while lying flat on her back. (And she *still* has no puckers!)

Frances never makes quilts to please the public; she chooses fabrics and designs that please her and make her feel good. She pays no attention to the colors and styles "of the moment," confident that her workmanship will never be out of style. She is right: her quilts are avidly sought by collectors from California to Florida who recognize their worth. Many have been willing to pay thousands of dollars for unquilted tops alone.

Quilts are not the only beautiful things Frances makes; to relax from her quilting labors, she crafts Fabergé-type eggs, modeled after those made by that gifted jeweler for the last czar of Russia. Using goose or rhea eggs, she fashions incredibly intricate designs, many of which contain pairs of doors so that a scene within may be disclosed. Some eggs are covered entirely with seed pearls; others have intricate filigree cutwork; a few are velvet-lined with hand-sculpted miniature figures inside; all are unbelievable. Only recently has she agreed to sell any of them. MACO now has some that are priced in the hundreds of dollars.

Frances and MACO Crafts have been good partners. MACO has had no trouble selling all the quilts Frances has placed with us. As part of our livelihood, we have, through the years, contracted with design firms in New York City to produce elaborate and sophisticated wall pieces for many corporate clients, among them Mobil Oil. These pieces were professionally stitched, awesome in their size and complexity, very expensive, and helped MACO build a reputation for excellence. All this, plus the cooperative's making of the original "World's Largest Quilt" notwithstanding, I must rank Frances Benton's "Baltimore Album Quilt" as the finest work of art to pass through MACO during our twenty-five years of existence.

I am grateful to Frances for sharing her talents and her friendship with me. Her quilts and her Fabergé eggs have brought me beauty and pleasure; her laughter and courage have brought joy and inspiration to my soul.

THE NEXT QUILT TOP IS A BALTIMORE ALBUM—I PLAN ON GOING A LITTLE CRAZY

August 7, 1991

Hello Margaret:

Enclosed is the letter you requested. Hope it has enough information to answer all the questions you get about me.

The next quilt top after the Bird Quilt is a Baltimore Album or Baltimore Bride. They are both such complicated patterns that I plan on going a little crazy.

Trying to figure out a way to get up there to see your fabrics, so far no luck. Any suggestions on what you have for Baltimores?

Sincerely,

Frances

• • •

$\mathcal{E}$ACH BLOCK HAS AT LEAST A HUNDRED PIECES

January 23, 1992

Hello Margaret:

There's 4' of snow on ground and cold as blue blazes.

I'm working on a top that allows no imagination but is pretty. Should be ready in about a month.

Busy as a cat on a roof setting up the Baltimore Album top. Have to wait to see if I have goofed. I think not, but the possibility is always there. Each block has at least a hundred pieces. There will be three-dimensional flowers plus other innovations I have never tried before. I am trying to stay in line with the antiques of yore, but pretty hard to do, as they were wrong quite a few times. (Tee, hee.) Twenty-five blocks—the flowered borders are ten inches wide—plus a border on each side of that. No more medallion styles like last three. I have to go back and say it might have a flowered border—a scalloped border would be in line—as the one K___ bought. After I put blocks together, I will know more.

If you will look through your *Quilter's Newsletter Magazine* #202, May 1988,

you will see what I am trying to do. It's on the front cover. This sold for $100 thousand.*

I have spent over $100 to research the Baltimore quilts, plus have have found some of the most beautiful fabric to some very weird. One clerk said, "Ms., I don't mean to insult you, but what on earth are you gonna do with this ugly stuff?"

I told her, and she still looked at me real peculiar. Then I told her how much my quilt tops sold for, and she finally gave me credit for having a little brains. Someone who sees fabric as I do, as a substitute for paint, knows that often you only use tiny pieces to detail a more realistic flower, etc. I would estimate I now have $500 in fabrics for the top.

This is one I would love so to quilt, and can't. There's so much wrong with me I sometimes wonder why I even try. Then I count my blessings. I wish I could visit with all of you, but I see no chance now. Maybe this top will be so

valuable I will have to deliver it by hand. Ha, ha. Sounds good anyway. All my news.

> Love,
> Frances

(The quilt the author refers to is dated 1848, and it was auctioned at Sotheby's New York for the second highest price ever paid for a quilt at that time. The highest price had been set in 1988, also at auction at Sotheby's, also for a Baltimore Album Quilt, which brought $176,000.)

. . .

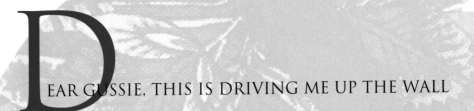

DEAR GUSSIE, THIS IS DRIVING ME UP THE WALL

May 4, 1992

Hello Margaret:

Here's that crazy lady again who likes a challenge, oops scratch that out, who used to meet a problem head on. This one knocked her down. Dear Gussie, this is driving me up the wall.

My absolute biggest problem is that I want to stay true to the concept of Baltimore Album quilts But some of the designs are so primitive, I couldn't make myself follow the rules.

So I went beyond compromise. I just gave up and made it my way in a lot of the blocks.

I bought fabric for six months before I even started the top, so in some cases I was bound and determined to use fabric whether it fit or not. I had to change and change again, over and over again. That is what eats up a lot of my time. I'm a Libra, so the decisions are hard to make anyway.

Margaret, my mind is so fouled up now, I'm trying to think what on earth I will do in the way of quilt tops when this is finished. I'm afraid everything else will seem unnecessary.

Some of the roses are three-dimensional. I have left petals loose so they can be quilted underneath, then tacked down after quilting. Some roses are to be quilted on the bottom petals, like so. (Diagram)

Enclosed are pictures of some of the blocks. Did not take too well. Rather washed out in color at top of photos. I am now sewing on 15th block. Ten more to go. Then the borders. Read back of photos.

Love.

Frances

• • •

We won't talk about this one. Just lock me up & throw away the key.

The silk on vase cost $35.00 a yard. I used a small square, only bought five small pieces.

This block is a jewel.

. . . The harp is made of suede fabric; I had to try to see if it could be done.

O FOOL LIKE AN OLD FOOL

July 15, 1992

Hello Margaret:

I'm still plugging along. Five more blocks to go. Then the border. So it looks like September at the earliest before finish! I have stopped griping and complaining and decided that I'm the one who started this thing, so I'll just finish it. No fool like an old fool. By the time I finish it I will hate it so much, I wouldn't give two cents for it.

What I really dread is the possibility that when I start on something less complicated I will really lose my mind through boredom.

I really didn't know what I was getting into on this one. It is so busy and three-dimensional that you can't do a good press job on it. So many fabrics you wonder if it's wise to use the blue pen to mark the quilting. Although I washed and pressed all the fabrics, you still get nervous about so many fabrics. Of course I don't worry about the pressing too much because once it is taut in the frame for quilting it will be okay.

Now, here's my problem. I need three yards of fabric (sample enclosed) for

border. I'm two months away from using it but thought I would start looking now. If you have it call me collect and I will send check.

How's the bird quilt going? Wish I could see it quilted.

Things here are about the same. Plenty of pain to go around. My hands are almost past the point of gripping the small needles. I have discovered exercises to stop some of the pain in my back and hips. I scream in pain during these exercises but when it's over, no more pain for at least two hours. Now that's good! All my news.

Love,

Frances

. . .

"HERE IT IS AND ISN'T IT BEAUTIFUL?"

September 7, 1992

Hello Margaret:

First, before you speak of this quilt top to anyone, maybe you should refer them to the Elly Sienkiewicz books on Baltimore Album quilts. I also used Jeana Kimball's books for reference. Some folks do not realize what these quilts were—in their time, they were strictly originals, so much so that now they appear very primitive. I suspect that in many cases, other than roses, these women had only wildflowers to copy.

Now, some comments about the construction. Freezer paper saved the day on this effort. I always iron the paper to the fabric, cut 3/16" away from paper, then baste the fabric to the paper. There are other methods, but I find this most accurate. These designs were so varied in shapes and colors that I basted all the pieces to the block before whipping them down. That way, I could be sure they all went together. Good thing I did, because there were many times I had to throw away and replace when colors did not please. Sometimes I even had to change the shape of flowers

and/or leaves. The 3-D roses will have to be quilted underneath, then petals tacked down.

I found several Christmas fabrics which had the most wonderful leaves, which let me make so many different leaves across the top. I was questioned many times by

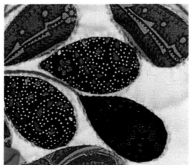

41

clerks who wanted to know what in the world I was going to do with this (uck) fabric. Now, about the gathered flowers, just don't ask. Almost lost my wits, but determination is my strong suit.

I left the words "The Album" off the book in the center of the quilt top, thinking that whoever bought it might want their name there.

Although this has been a trial and tribulation to make, I must say I have enjoyed the challenge. I also remembered what our foremothers went through to produce their wonderful quilts. It was an age of rub boards, clothes lines, wood cook stoves, six or more kids and little money. My word! What they had left in the way of sanity went into these things of beauty. I weep for them even today. They had no freezer paper, no masking tape, no electric iron, very few pins, one needle for everything. I feel ashamed every time I think about the times I cussed while making my top. Ha, ha. I have read that in the West around 1850 a white woman was killed by an Indian woman because she would not give up her needle. Imagine that! I guess that Indian figured that she would not have to chew a hide so much if she had a steel needle that would penetrate the hide instead of a bone needle that would not. Here we are today, reaching back into history to duplicate the work of these women who left a legacy they never dreamed of. It boggles the mind.

I hope someone appreciates my work as much as I appreciate those who came before me. Their designs, my work.

The top is 110" X 110". Name: Baltimore Album. I have no idea what it is worth. Margaret, let's talk about that. I am too far removed from the quilt market to know what is going on. The making of it used up my brain capacity anyway.

The border is part of one in the Jeana Kimball book on borders. The green points are from the suggestions from the Elly book *Baltimore Beauties and Beyond, Volume 2*," (green cover), first color page (81). When the top was finished, it took me three days to come back down from pushing so hard. I felt better when I was working on it if I did nothing else, *i.e.*, I allowed nothing else to distract me. Now I walk around in circles trying to decide what to do next. I'm sure I will focus after a little time passes. All I can say now is, "Here it is and isn't it beautiful?"

Love always,

Frances

• • •

I AM GONNA QUILT THAT SUCKER

January 25, 1993

Hello Margaret:

Enclosed is the magazine we discussed. Page 4 gives the description and price. My borders are shown in Elly's books.

I wonder if you should mention that I'm trying to make the deadline for the Baltimore Quilt Contest that C&T Publishers in California is running in October? I don't care about the prize money, just the prestige of winning. I would like to have a non-monetary prize. I don't have regulations yet, will mail off for them.

I'm glad you have someone interested in buying the Baltimore Album Quilt. Would they like a name on the Album book in the quilt top?

I guess you can say, yes, I will quilt it. I just have to work up a schedule of two hours at the frame, one hour off, and work exercise into time off. The split hours are a pest but that's all I can think of. I can also adjust my insulin. In any case, I am gonna quilt that sucker.

Frances

· · ·

"...YOU WON'T HAVE TO QUILT THE DARN THING"

March 24, 1993

Hi Margaret:

You are reading a letter from a very scared person. I've never seen such a large quilt. Ha ha. If I had only known I would have to quilt it! I remember thinking as I was making the top, "Oh, go ahead and put such and so on the thing, you won't have to quilt the darn thing. Ha! I have it in the frame, started quilting last night. Everything is gradually coming back to me. It's been 10 years.* Pray for me.

Love,

Frances

*(It had been that long since Frances had actually quilted a piece. She had been delivering only the appliquéd tops, unquilted, to MACO.)

• • •

THIS HUGE BLANK SPACE THAT IS NOT QUILTED

April 10, 1993

Hello Margaret:

You do know this Baltimore Album is a one-time quilt job, don't you? Don't ask about which one will I quilt next. This is it! Dear Gussie, I have never quilted so much and got no where, tee hee. I leave the frame for an hour, then return to this huge blank space that is not quilted, and I sit down, take a deep breath and laugh at myself. That's good, huh?

I do know now why I had to stop quilting, though. It's a good thing other quilters like my tops to quilt for themselves. Just think of all those tops that I have made all these years. I do know I cannot stay at the frame long enough to make quilting plausible. Will let you know if I proceed to insanity in the near future. If you don't hear from me, write me a letter...Ha ha.

Love ya

Frances

• • •

$\mathcal{S}$OME THOUGHTS ON ADDICTION

May 2, 1993

Hello Margaret:

I'm still here, barely. I ignored the arthritic pain until it no longer made sense. I stopped for three days. Now I'm back in the swing of it again. I've been sitting at the frame thinking about my joining MACO and being afraid my quilts would not be up to your standards. I have never, anywhere, been made to feel so welcome.

Thank you. If my quilts had not been up to par, you would have let me down so gently I would not have felt the bump.

I thought of the quilt show right after I joined MACO. I walked up behind a woman standing in front of one of my quilts arguing with herself out loud as to whether the quilt was quilted by hand or machine. I thanked her very much.

You would be surprised at the number of store clerks I bought fabric from who have come by to see this Baltimore in progress. I was asked many times what I would use this or that for. If I bought a half-yard, I would probably use only two inches—I

was after that certain color. This fascinated them. Of course, I ordered off to *Quilter's Newsletter Magazine* for quite a lot of Jenny Beyer's prints, and as you know, I bought the yardage for the red border from MACO, which was one of Jenny Beyer's fabrics by R.J. Reynolds.

One of the women wanted to know why I made quilts. She was referring to the amount of work involved. That is when I went into my litany of being addicted after the first one I made. It is not work, it's an addiction. You don't get discouraged enough to quit, you are addicted. I have enough quilts in my brain to last two lifetimes. I hurry, knowing I will never catch up. That's the addiction. I have been asked how I could sell one after so much work involved. I jokingly replied, "I can't affored one of my quilts." But it really was true.

But just think of this: look how many more tops I can make if I don't quilt. I can get rid of more of the quilts in my brain. There have been times when I have set up four or five tops at one time, then I would wonder which one to work on next. There have been times when I passed all those up and did another one on impulse.

I better close this down. I was due back at the frame long ago.

Love,

Frances

P.S. Tired but undaunted.

• • •

AVERAGING 8 HOURS A DAY, SOMETIMES 10

May 30, 1993

Hello Margaret:

I am still glued to the quilting frame. I am averaging eight hours a day, sometimes ten. When you try for 12 to 16 stitches per inch, you don't move over the quilt very fast. I worried for a while about my stitches being even, then thought, "Don't worry about it, just make them too small to see." Ha ha.

I meant to ask what you thought about different colored thread showing through on the lining, because I insist on matching thread to fabric color on the quilt top. I have heard pros and cons on this, but I always come to the conclusion that this is what I want to do, because it pleases me.

I'd like to tell you how much longer I'll be quilting, but from this acre I see from here, who knows? All my news.

Love ya,

Frances

I AM NOW QUILTING ON LAST ROW OF BLOCKS... I AM NOW ON LAST OF BORDER

June 14, 1993

Hello Margaret:

I'm still kicking, but not very high. I'm now looking at the end of the quilt. Two more turns and it's out of the frame. I'm picking up speed, because I have learned to work my hands with hard exercise to limber them up before starting.

You know I was thinking about the remark I made to the woman about why I sold my quilts and thought I sounded rather flip. The reason I sell, I guess, is because I see no reason to keep them. Also, it allows me to purchase more fabric and make the ones my brain won't let me forget.

I am now quilting on last row of blocks. I can hardly wait to get it out of the frame and see how it looks overall.

Everyone keeps watching me to see if I'll fall out of my chair. I roll under the frame to do exercises and my little Lhasa Apso licks and chews till I have to get up.

I am now on last of border: this letter has been a long slow one. It is now 5 a.m.

and the house is quiet, so I will quilt two hours, then breakfast. By that time, the pain will be humming. By the way, I haven't mentioned this, but I do use adhesive tape on the finger under the quilt. It still gets sore as a boil, but so what? Pain is nothing new.

I can stick out my chest now, "IT" is almost finished.

Well, will quit for now and go for the last of the stitches.

Love,

Frances

• • •

I HAVE NEVER BEFORE SEEN A BALTIMORE ALBUM QUILT IN PERSON

June 30, 1993

Dear Margaret:

Guess what? Remember when I sent you the top and thought it was so beautiful? I didn't think it would be possible to feel this way after it was quilted. I am completely overcome. I have seen many different pictures of Baltimore Album quilts, but never one in person. No wonder they are considered the ultimate in the quilt world. It is gorgeous. Not just because it's my work. It's the variety of the blocks, the intense riot of color. No matter where you put the blocks, they all come together. I worried about having them make sense, when no two tied together in any way. Imagine this, they don't have to tie together. I feel very humble when I think of our foremothers putting something like this together. What a legacy they left us, even though they had so little to work with.

Well, girl, it is now finished, and the quilting frame is in the garage being made into something else. And I am walking around like a war casualty in shock.

I will bring it to you in about two weeks. I've got to find something else to do. Remember I have been wrapped up in this for one and a half years.

Frances

• • •

SUGGESTED READING

If you are interested in learning more about Baltimore Album Quilts, the following publications are recommended.

The Magazine Antiques, March 1994, vol. CXLV, No.3: New York, N.Y.: Brant Publications. 1994. pp. 412-421. "Baltimore Album Quilts," by Jennifer F. Goldsborough.

Ms. Goldsborough was the chief curator of the Maryland Historical Society in Baltimore. Her text is concerned primarily with the question of the identities of the designers of Baltimore Album quilts, and the glorious full-color photographs she provides as examples of the different design styles are from the Historical Society's extensive collection as well as from private sources.

Uncoverings 1994: The Journal of the American Quilt Study Group. San Francisco, California. 1995. "An Album of Baltimore Album Quilt Studies," by Jennifer F. Goldsborough.

In planning the 1994 exhibition of its Baltimore album quilt collection, "Lavish Legacies: Baltimore Album Quilts 1845-1855," the Maryland Historical Society gathered a diverse group of scholars to research these extraordinary textiles in as wide a variety of ways as possible. This paper delineates the methodology of the study and the contributions of several sorts of historians, curators, conservators, and contemporary quilters. The cooperative and collegial nature of the study resulted in exciting new findings and conclusions concerning where, when, by whom, and under what conditions these marvelous and sumptous quilts were made.

Appliqué Borders: An Added Grace, and *Reflections of Baltimore*, both by Jeana Kimball. (That Patchwork Place; Bothell, Washington; 1991 and 1989.)

Ms. Kimball's book on borders contains easy-to-use full-size patterns for sixteen original appliqué border designs printed on oversize sheets. "Very helpful," says Frances. "Those oversize sheets are just wonderful. I used the swags, corners, and bows from the pattern named 'Double Swag' on page 11."

The author says of *Reflections of Baltimore*, "Using the Baltimore Album Quilt as inspiration, I drew and stitched quilt blocks that pleased me. The techniques I used are described in this book. Quality is timeless, and so it is with these quilts. They are as appealing today as they were at the time of their origin." The book contains thirteen block patterns, some of which provided inspiration for Frances.

The American Quilt, A History of Cloth and Comfort, 1750-1950, by Roderick Kiracofe and Mary Elizabeth Johnson. (Clarkson Potter; New York; 1993.)

Contained within the text of this comprehensive history of quilting in the United States are essays on Friendship Album Quilts and Baltimore Album Quilts. The sociological factors affecting the emergence of these two related styles of quiltmaking are discussed, and lovely color photographs of heretofore unseen examples are given. Especially interesting is a pair of Baltimore Album-type quilts said to have been made by different generations of the same family twenty-five years apart.

Books by Elly Sienkiewicz:

Spoken Without a Word–A Lexicon of Selected Symbols With 24 Patterns from Classic Baltimore Album Quilts (1983).

This was the first book to faithfully reproduce patterns from classic Baltimore Album Quilts and to point out the intentional symbolism within these quilts' design motifs.

Baltimore Beauties and Beyond, Studies in Classic Album Quilt Appliqué, Volume I (1989).

Twelve lessons take the beginner from the simplest Baltimore Album Quilt blocks to the most complex. Appliqué techniques are presented and 24 Album blocks are given.

Baltimore Album Quilts, Historic Notes and Antique Patterns, A Pattern Companion to Baltimore Beauties and Beyond, Volume I (1990).

56 patterns offer the framework for sharing Baltimore's fascinating historical saga and closeup pictures of antique blocks and albums.

Baltimore Beauties and Beyond, Studies in Classic Album Quilt Appliqué, Volume II (1991).

This volume pictures more than 50 antebellum Albums and offers 20 block and 13 border patterns.

Appliqué 12 Easy Ways! Charming Quilts, Giftable Projects, and Timeless Techniques (1991).

A very basic how-to-appliqué book illustrated with wonderful clarity. Complete patterns include 29 projects from gifts to graphic museum replica quilts.

Design a Baltimore Album Quilt, A Design Companion to Volume II of Baltimore Beauties and Beyond, Studies in Classic Album Quilt Appliqué (1992).

This book gives directions on planning the set and borders of a Baltimore Album Quilt, as well as instructions for how to make several antique bindings and all the patterns, including a border, for a 25-block antique Baltimore Album Quilt.

Dimensional Appliqué—A Pattern Companion to Volume II of Baltimore Beauties and Beyond, Studies in Classic Album Quilt Appliqué (1993).

Simple, innovative methods for dimensional flowers and unique appliqué basketry.

Baltimore Album Revival! Historic Quilts in the Making—Catalog of C&T Publishing's Baltimore Revival Quilt Show and Contest (1994).

This catalog documents a historic exhibition and contains an essay as insightful as it is entertaining, analyzing why Baltimore-style Album Quilts have become so popular again.

Appliqué 12 Borders and Medallions! A Pattern Companion to Volume III of Baltimore Beauties and Beyond, Studies in Classic Album Quilt Appliqué (1994).

Here are a dozen patterns fully drafted and pictured in fabric for some of the most beautiful fruit and floral borders in the classic Albums.

Papercuts and Plenty, Volume III of Baltimore Beauties and Beyond, Studies in Classic Album Quilt Appliqué (1995).

Paper-cut appliqué albums have always been the author's favorite stylistic stream in the antebellum Baltimores. Dirctions for this surprisingly expressive style plus intriguing lessons on "Fabulous Fruits" are included.

Stitched in Cloth, Carved in Stone, A Sequel to Volume III of Baltimore Beauties and Beyond, Studies in Classic Album Quilt Appliqué (1997).

This book will bring the author's study of symbols in the Albums full circle. It will include a guide to the fraternal symbols which permeated Victorian decorative arts. A fascinating selection of photographs will illustrate these symbols stitched on quilts in cloth and carved in grave markers in stone. Included in this final volume will be a historical analysis of what caused the Baltimore Albums to bloom so profusely, who made these famous quilts, why the style spread so widely, and what brought the Album era to an end.

With the exception of her first, self-published book, all of Ms. Sienkiewicz's books are available from C&T Publishing, P.O. Box 1456, Lafayette, CA 94549. Her first book is available from Vermont Patchworks, Box 229, Shrewsbury, VT 05738.

CREATED BY

Frances

Benton

1993

BORN 9-25-22